People

Families

by Sarah L. Schuette

Consulting Editor: Gail Saunders-Smith, PhD

Capstone
press

Mankato, Minnesota

Pebble Books are published by Capstone Press,
1710 Roe Crest Drive, North Mankato, Minnesota 56003.
www.capstonepub.com

Library of Congress Cataloging-in-Publication Data
Schuette, Sarah L., 1976–
      Families / by Sarah L. Schuette. — Rev. and updated ed.
      p. cm. — (Pebble books. People)
      Includes bibliographical references and index.
      Summary: "In simple text and photos, presents families and what family
members do" — Provided by publisher.
      ISBN-13: 978-1-4296-2239-4 (hardcover)
      ISBN-10: 1-4296-2239-3 (hardcover)
      ISBN-13: 978-1-4296-3462-5 (softcover)
      ISBN-10: 1-4296-3462-6 (softcover)
1. Family — Juvenile literature. I. Title. II. Series.
HQ744.S38 2009
306.85 — dc22   2008026951

Printed in the United States of America in Eau Claire, Wisconsin.
092013   007714R

Note to Parents and Teachers

The People set supports national social studies standards related
to individual development and identity. This book describes
and illustrates families. The images support early readers in
understanding the text. The repetition of words and phrases helps
early readers learn new words. This book also introduces early
readers to subject-specific vocabulary words, which are defined
in the Glossary section. Early readers may need assistance to read
some words and to use the Table of Contents, Glossary, Read More,
Internet Sites, and Index sections of the book.

Table of Contents

Families

Families are people
related to one another.
There are all kinds
of families.

Some family members
live close together.
Other family members
live far away.

Family Fun

Families enjoy
being together.
Art and his father
look for bugs.

Juan and his mother
eat ice cream.

Audrey and her sister jump rope.

Matt and his grandparents toast marshmallows.

Grace and her uncle play golf.

Mia and her cousins
go bowling.

Loving Families

Families love.

They take care

of each other.

Glossary

cousin — the children of your aunt or uncle

father — a male parent

grandparent — the parent of your mother or father; grandmothers and grandfathers are grandparents.

mother — a female parent

related — to be part of the same family

uncle — your mother or father's brother

Read More

Adamson, Heather. *Families in Many Cultures.* Life around the World. Mankato, Minn.: Capstone Press, 2007.

Easterling, Lisa. *Families.* Our Global Community. Chicago: Heinemann, 2007.

Gallagher, Debbie. *Family Members.* Families. New York: Marshall Cavendish Benchmark, 2008.

Internet Sites

FactHound offers a safe, fun way to find educator-approved Internet sites related to this book.

Here's what you do:
1. Visit www.facthound.com
2. Choose your grade level.
3. Begin your search.

This book's ID number is 9781429622394.

FactHound will fetch the best sites for you!

Index

Word Count: 75
Grade: 1
Early-Intervention Level: 12

Credits
Abbey Fitzgerald, designer; Marcy Morin, photo shoot scheduler

Photo Credits
Capstone Press/Karon Dubke, all

The author dedicates this book to the memory of her cousin,
    Derrick Thomas Schmidt and in honor of his parents,
    Terry and Jenny Schmidt of Belle Plaine, Minnesota.